EASY GUITAR
WITH NOTES & TAB

CHART HITS OF 2016-2017

ISBN 978-1-4950-9063-9

7777 W. BLUEMOUND RD. P.O. BOX 13819 MILWAUKEE, WI 53213

Visit Hal Leonard Online at
www.halleonard.com

STRUM AND PICK PATTERNS

This chart contains the suggested strum and pick patterns that are referred to by number at the beginning of each song in this book. The symbols ⊓ and ∨ in the strum patterns refer to down and up strokes, respectively. The letters in the pick patterns indicate which right-hand fingers play which strings.

p = thumb
i = index finger
m = middle finger
a = ring finger

For example; Pick Pattern 2
is played: thumb - index - middle - ring

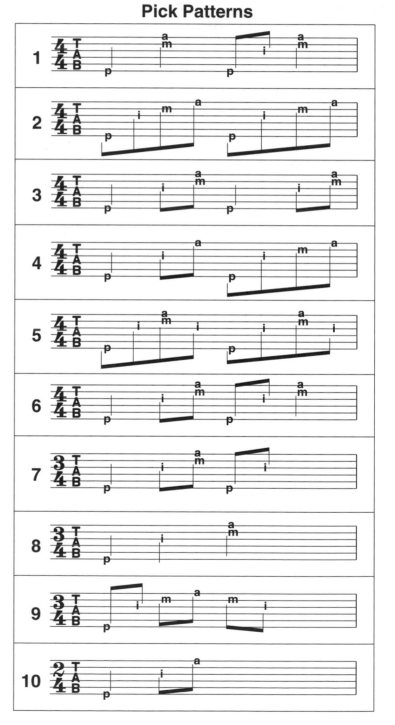

Strum Patterns   ## Pick Patterns

You can use the 3/4 Strum and Pick Patterns in songs written in compound meter (6/8, 9/8, 12/8, etc.). For example, you can accompany a song in 6/8 by playing the 3/4 pattern twice in each measure. The 4/4 Strum and Pick Patterns can be used for songs written in cut time (¢) by doubling the note time values in the patterns. Each pattern would therefore last two measures in cut time.

Heathens

from SUICIDE SQUAD

Words and Music by Tyler Joseph

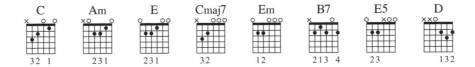

Strum Pattern: 1
Pick Pattern: 5

Chorus
Moderately

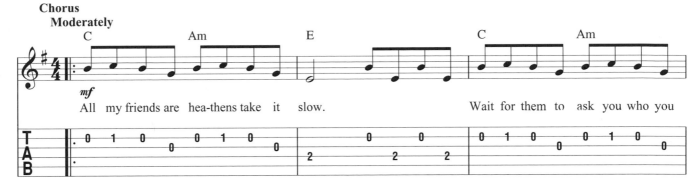

All my friends are hea-thens take it slow. Wait for them to ask you who you

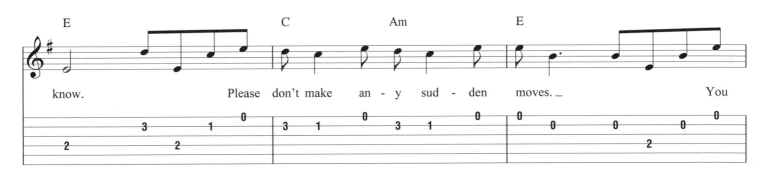

know. Please don't make an-y sud-den moves. ___ You

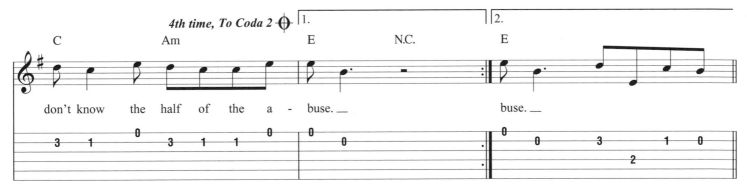

don't know the half of the a - buse. ___ buse. ___

Verse

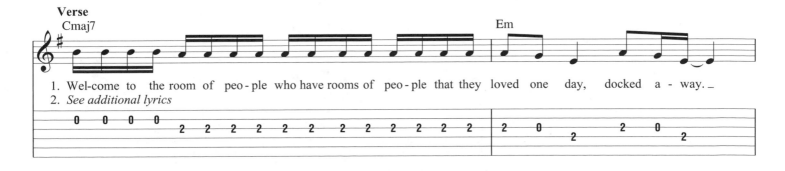

1. Wel-come to the room of peo-ple who have rooms of peo-ple that they loved one day, docked a - way. ___
2. *See additional lyrics*

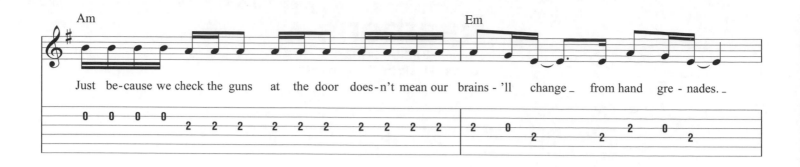

Just be-cause we check the guns at the door does-n't mean our brains-'ll change from hand gre-nades.

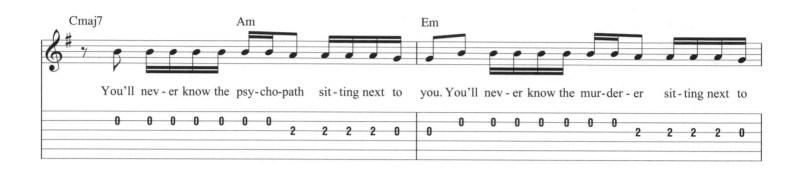

You'll nev-er know the psy-cho-path sit-ting next to you. You'll nev-er know the mur-der-er sit-ting next to

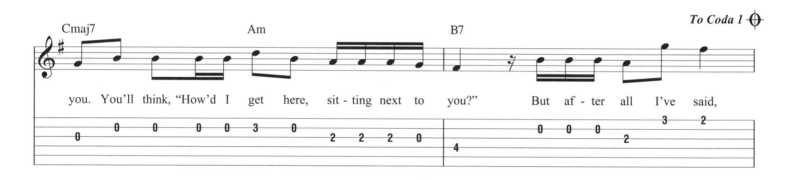

To Coda 1

you. You'll think, "How'd I get here, sit-ting next to you?" But af-ter all I've said,

Coda 1

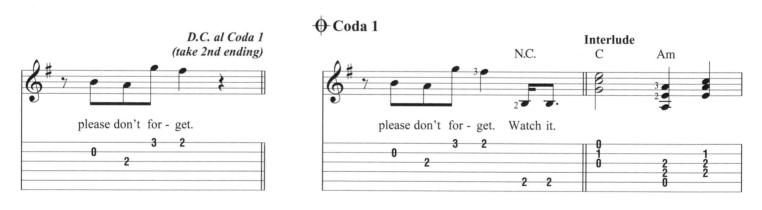

D.C. al Coda 1
(take 2nd ending)

please don't for - get.

Interlude

please don't for - get. Watch it.

Coda 2

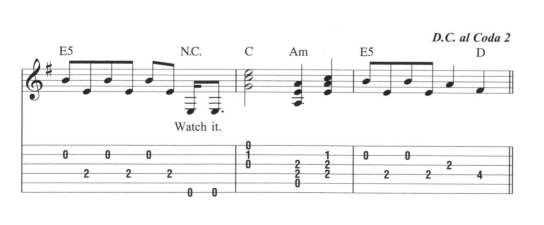

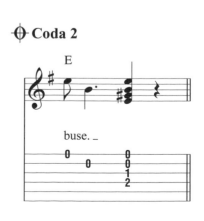

D.C. al Coda 2

Watch it.

buse.

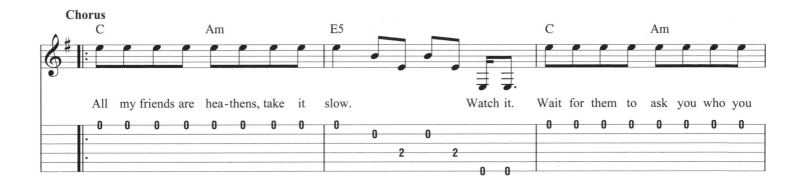

All my friends are hea-thens, take it slow. Watch it. Wait for them to ask you who you

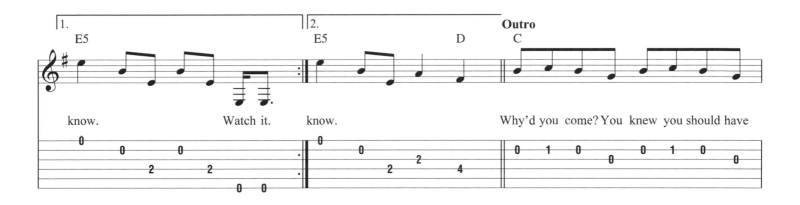

|1.

know.   Watch it.   know.   Why'd you come? You knew you should have

|2.   **Outro**

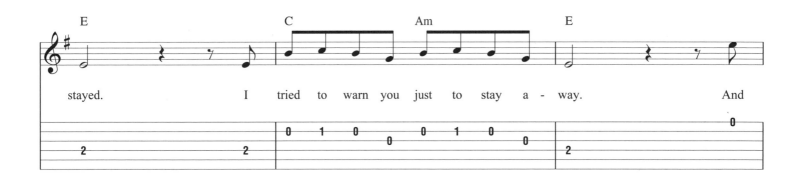

stayed.   I   tried to warn you just   to   stay   a - way.   And

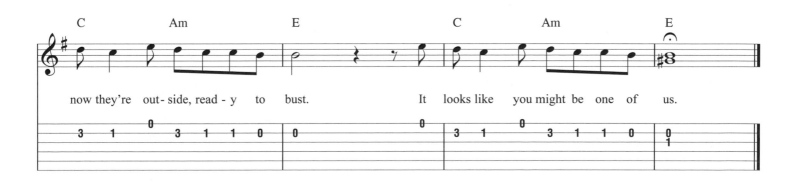

now they're out-side, read-y   to   bust.   It   looks like   you might be one of   us.

Additional Lyrics

2. We don't deal with outsiders very well. They say newcomers have a certain smell.
You have trust issues, not to mention, they say they can smell your intentions.
You'll never know the freak show sitting next to you. You'll have some weird people sitting next to you.
You'll think, "How did I get here, sitting next to you?"
But after all I've said, please don't forget. Watch it.

Closer

Words and Music by Andrew Taggart, Isaac Slade, Joseph King,
Ashley Frangipane, Shaun Frank and Frederic Kennett

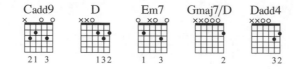

*Capo I

Strum Pattern: 3
Pick Pattern: 3

Intro
Moderately, in 2

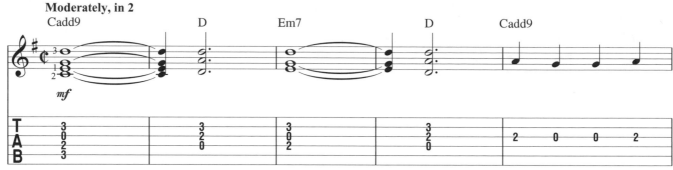

*Optional: To match recording, place capo at 1st fret.

1. Hey,
2. *See additional lyrics*

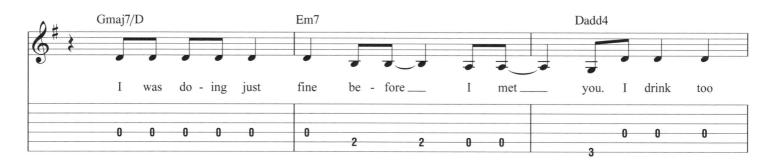

I was do-ing just fine be-fore ___ I met ___ you. I drink too

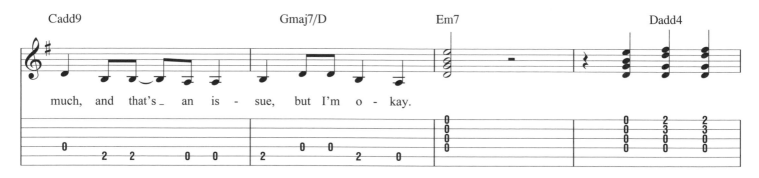

much, and that's ___ an is-sue, but I'm o-kay.

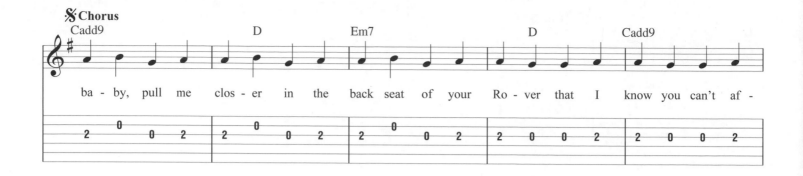

%Chorus

ba - by, pull me clos - er in the back seat of your Ro - ver that I know you can't af -

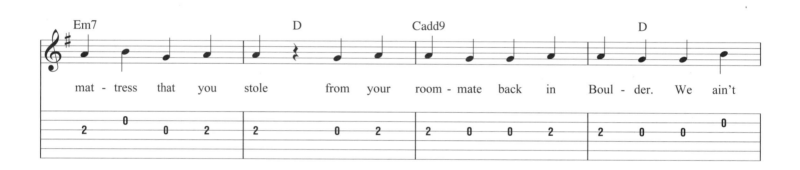

ford. Bite that tat - too on your should-der, pull the sheets right off the cor - ner of the

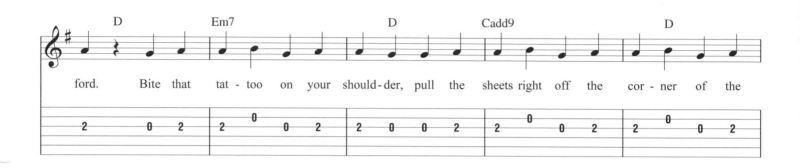

mat - tress that you stole from your room - mate back in Boul - der. We ain't

To Coda ⊕

Interlude

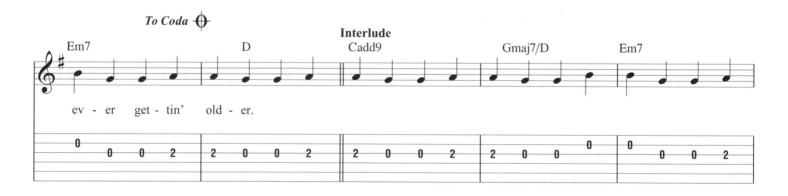

ev - er get - tin' old - er.

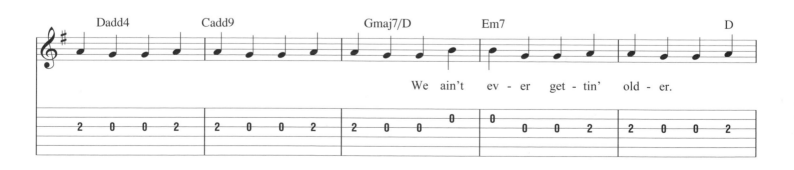

We ain't ev - er get - tin' old - er.

Additional Lyrics

2. You look as good as the day I met you.
I forget just why I left you; I was insane.
Stay, and play that Blink One-Eighty Two song
That we beat to death in Tuscon, okay?

Don't Wanna Know

Words and Music by Adam Levine, Benjamin Levin, John Henry Ryan, Ammar Malik, Jacob Kasher Hindlin, Alex Ben-Abdallah, Kendrick Lamar, Kurtis McKenzie and Jon Mills

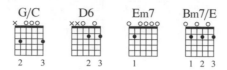

Strum Pattern: 6, 1
Pick Pattern: 6

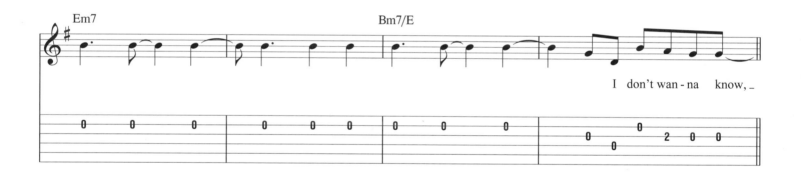

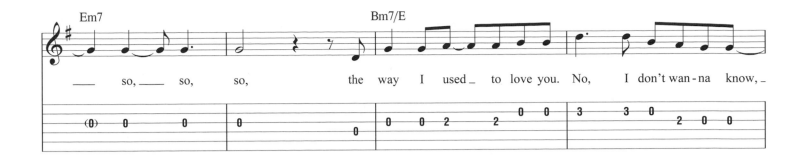

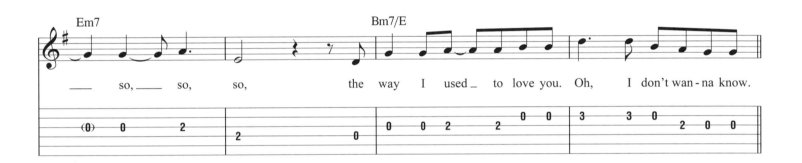

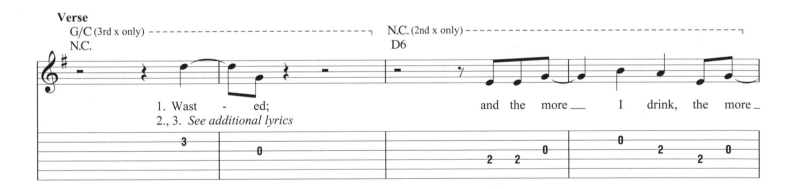

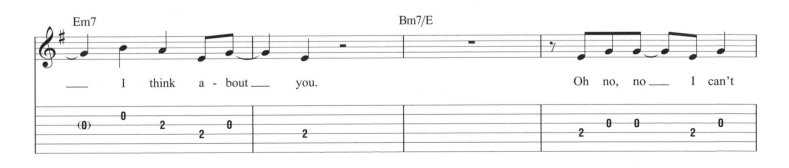

Additional Lyrics

2. And every time I got out, yeah,
   I hear it from this one, hear it from that one,
   That you got someone new, yeah.
   I see, but don't believe it.
   Even in my head, you're still in my bed.
   Maybe I'm just a fool.

3. Wasted, and the more I drink
   The more I think about you.
   Oh no, no I can't take it.
   Do you think that I should just go on without you?

I Don't Wanna Live Forever
(Fifty Shades Darker)

from FIFTY SHADES DARKER

Words and Music by Taylor Swift, Jack Antonoff and Sam Dew

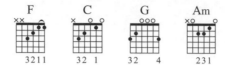

Strum Pattern: 5, 1
Pick Pattern: 5, 1

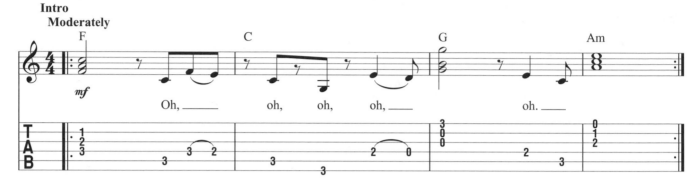

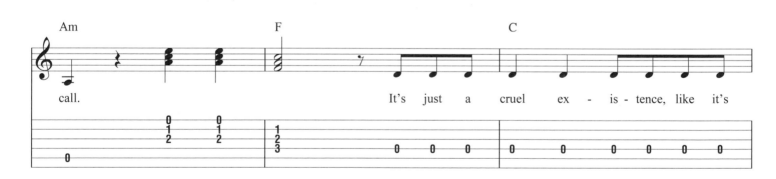

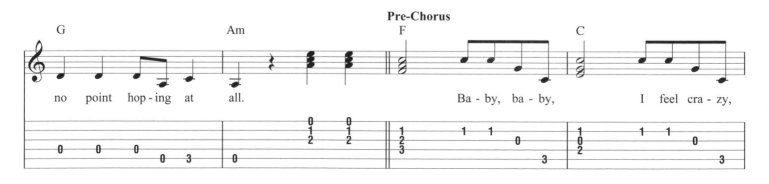

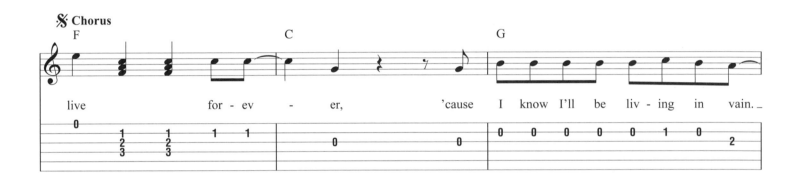

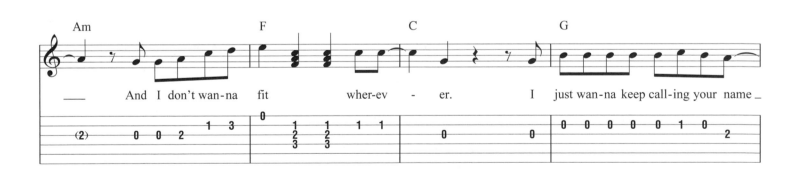

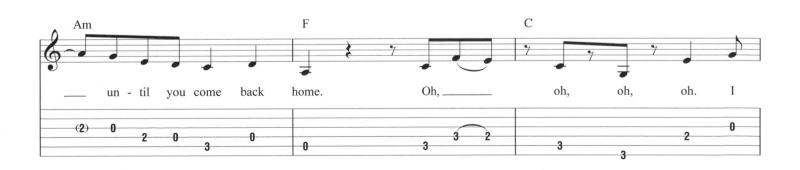

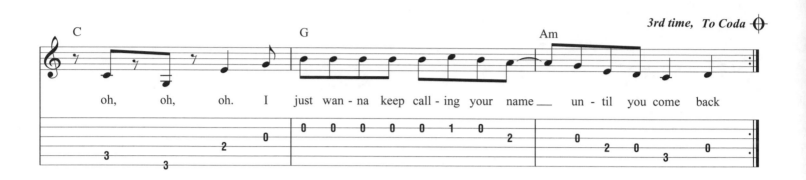

3rd time, To Coda

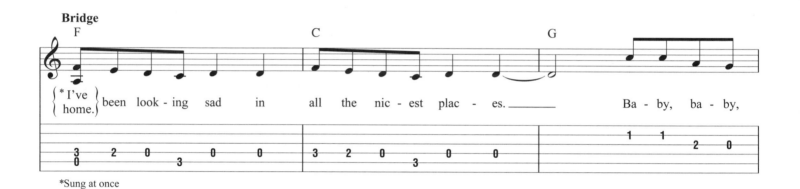

Bridge

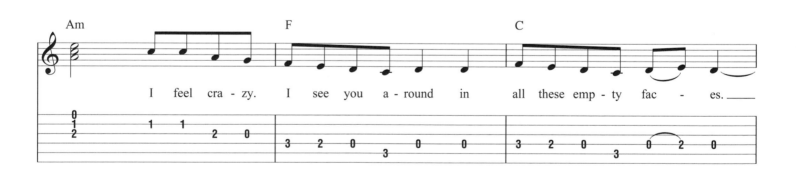

*Sung at once

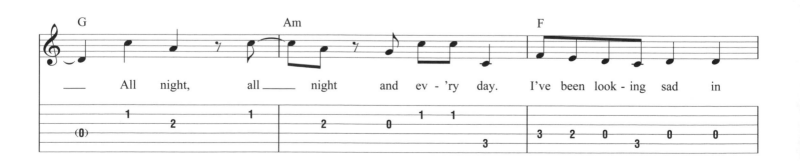

16

Additional Lyrics

2. I'm sitting eyes wide open,
   And I got one thing stuck in my mind:
   Wond'ring if I dodged a bullet
   Or just lost the love of my life.

I Took a Pill in Ibiza

Words and Music by Mike Posner

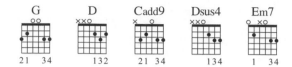

*Capo III

Strum Pattern: 3, 4
Pick Pattern: 1, 4

Intro
Moderately slow, in 2

*Optional: To match recording, place capo at 3rd fret

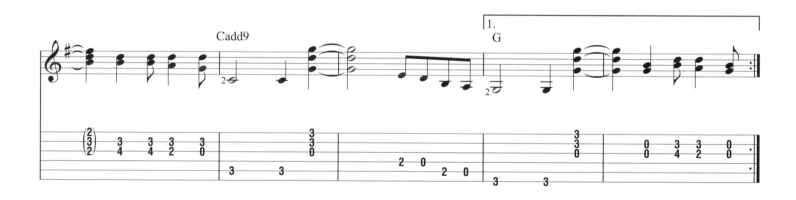

1. I took a pill in I- bi- za to show A-
2., 3. *See additional lyrics*

vi - cii I ___ was cool. And when I fi - n'lly got so - ber, felt ten years old - er, but

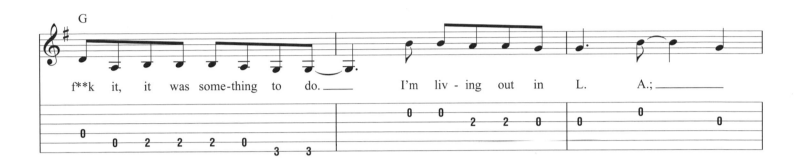

f**k it, it was some - thing to do. ___ I'm liv - ing out in L. A.; ___

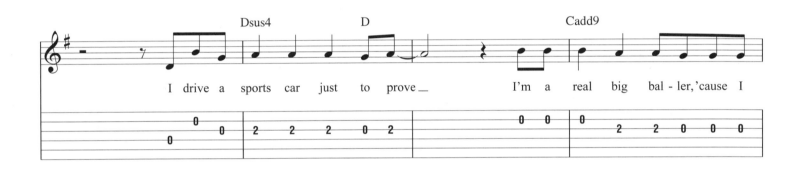

I drive a sports car just to prove ___ I'm a real big bal - ler, 'cause I

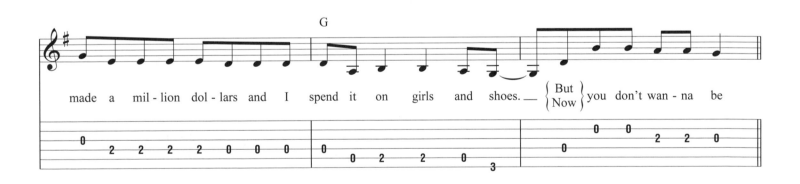

made a mil - lion dol - lars and I spend it on girls and shoes. ___ {But / Now} you don't wan - na be

Pre-Chorus

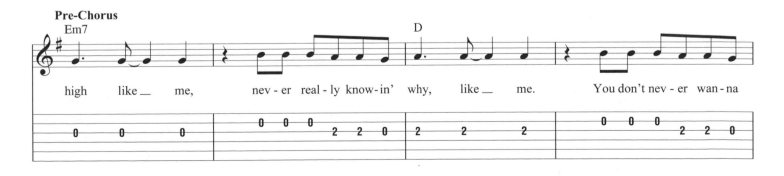

high like ___ me, nev - er real - ly know - in' why, like ___ me. You don't nev - er wan - na

step off that rol - ler coast - er and be all a - lone ___

And you don't wan - na ride the bus like ___ this, nev - er know - in' who to

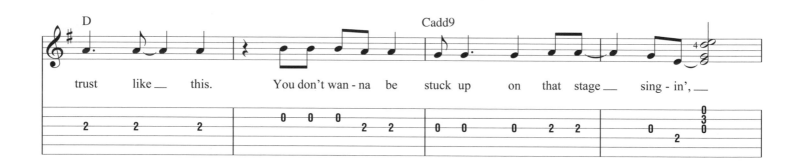

trust like ___ this. You don't wan - na be stuck up on that stage ___ sing - in', ___

Chorus

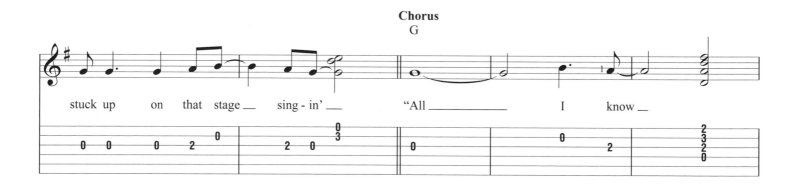

stuck up on that stage ___ sing - in' ___ "All _____ I know ___

are sad songs, ___ sad songs." ___ Dar - ling,

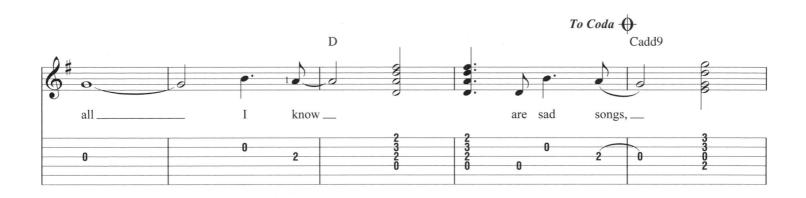

To Coda ⊕

D   Cadd9

all _____ I know __   are sad songs, __

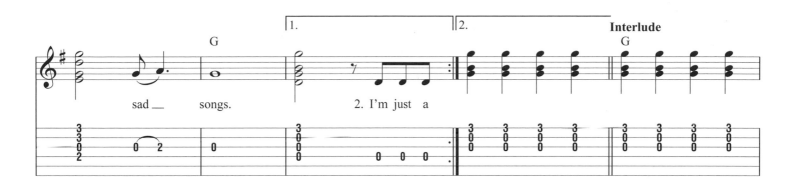

1.   2.   **Interlude**

G   G

sad __ songs.   2. I'm just a

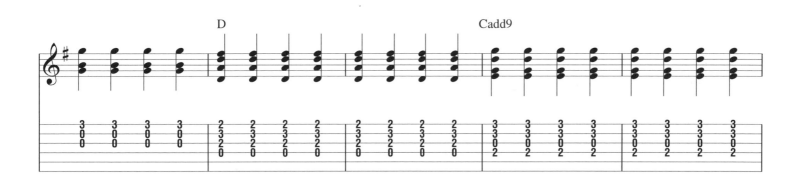

D   Cadd9

⊕ **Coda**

D.S. al Coda

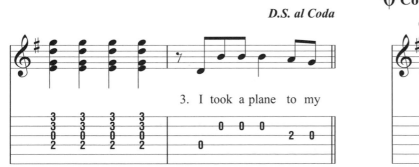

3. I took a plane to my

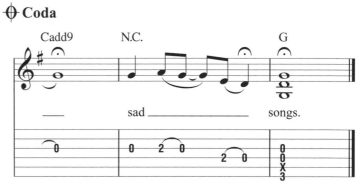

Cadd9   N.C.   G

__ sad _____ songs.

Additional Lyrics

2. I'm just a singer who already blew his shot.
   I get along with old timers 'cause my name's a reminder of a pop song people forgot.
   And I can't keep a girl, no; 'cause as soon a the sun comes up,
   I cut 'em all loose, and work's my excuse; but the truth is I can't open up.

3. I took a plane to my home town; I brought my pride and my guitar.
   Well, my friends are all gone, but there's manicured lawns, and the people still think I'm a star.
   I walked around downtown; I met some fans on Lafayette.
   They said, "Tell us how to make it 'cause we're getting real impatient."
   So I looked 'em in the eye and said…

Love on the Weekend

Words and Music by John Mayer

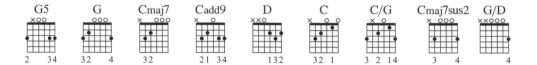

G5   G   Cmaj7   Cadd9   D   C   C/G   Cmaj7sus2   G/D

Strum Pattern: 5, 1
Pick Pattern: 1

Intro
Moderately

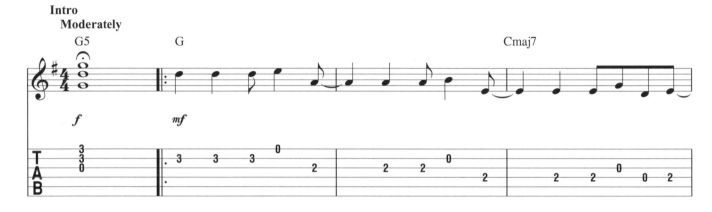

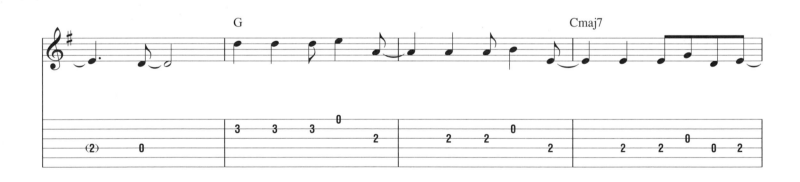

§ Verse

1. It's a Fri - day; we fi - n'lly made it.
2. You be the D. J.; I'll be the driv - er.
3. *See additional lyrics*

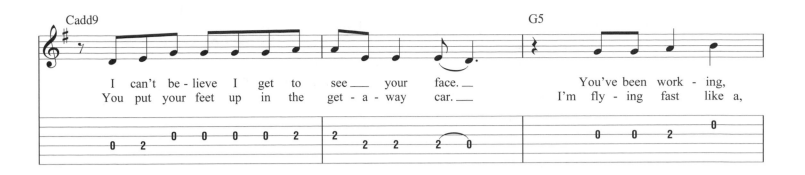

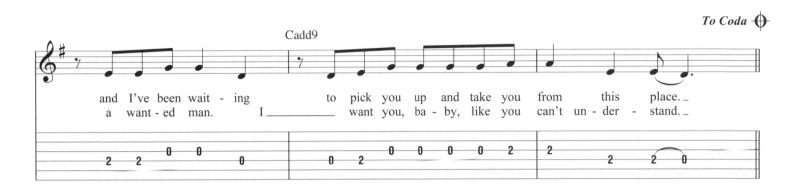

To Coda ⊕

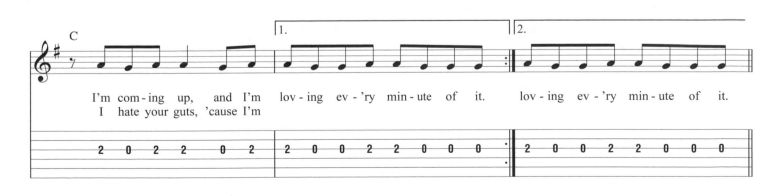

Bridge

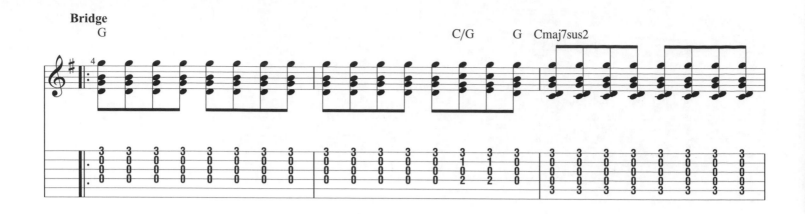

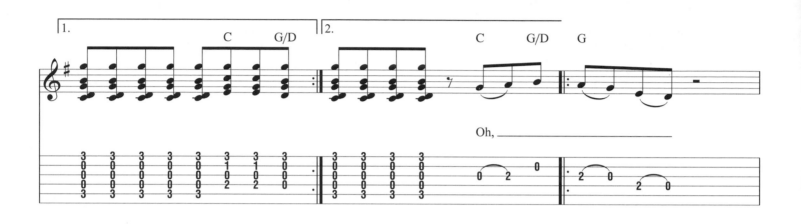

Oh, _____

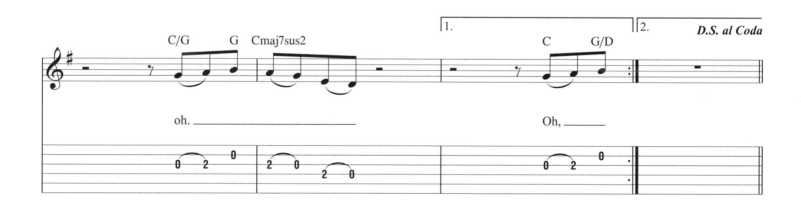

oh. _____

Oh, _____

D.S. al Coda

Coda

Chorus

And I'll be dream-ing of the next time we can go ___ in-to an-oth-er ser-o-

to - nin o - ver - flow. Love on the week - end, love on the week - end. __

I'm bust - ed up, but I'm lov - ing ev - 'ry min - ute of it.

Outro

Cmaj7

Repeat and fade

Love on __ the week - end. _____

Additional Lyrics

3. I gotta leave ya; it's gonna hurt me.
My clothes are dirty and my friends are worried.
Down there below us, under the clouds,
Baby, take my hand and pull me down, down, down, down.

Million Reasons

Words and Music by Stefani Germanotta, Mark Ronson and Hillary Lindsey

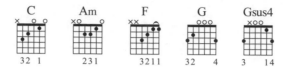

Strum Pattern: 5
Pick Pattern: 6, 1

Intro
Moderately slow, in 2

1. You're

Verse

giv - in' me a mil - lion rea - sons to let you go. ___ You're giv - in' me a mil - lion rea - sons
2. Head stuck in a cy - cle, I look off and I stare. ___ It's like that I've stopped breath - in' but com -

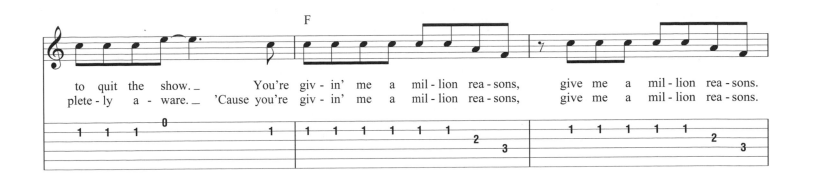

to quit the show. _____ You're giv - in' me a mil - lion rea - sons, give me a mil - lion rea - sons.
plete - ly a - ware. ___ 'Cause you're giv - in' me a mil - lion rea - sons, give me a mil - lion rea - sons.

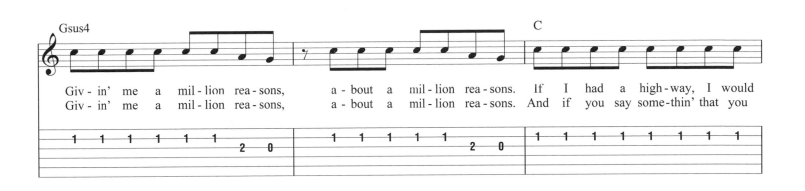

Giv - in' me a mil - lion rea - sons, a - bout a mil - lion rea - sons. If I had a high - way, I would
Giv - in' me a mil - lion rea - sons, a - bout a mil - lion rea - sons. And if you say some - thin' that you

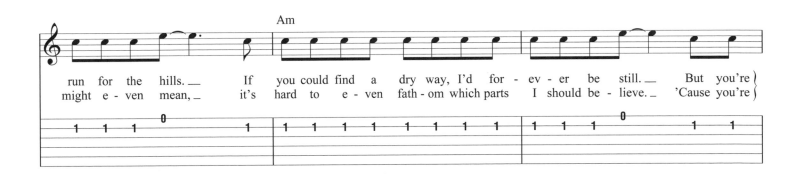

run for the hills. ___ If you could find a dry way, I'd for - ev - er be still. ___ But you're
might e - ven mean, ___ it's hard to e - ven fath - om which parts I should be - lieve. ___ 'Cause you're

giv - in' me a mil - lion rea - sons, give me a mil - lion rea - sons. Giv - in' me a mil - lion rea - sons,

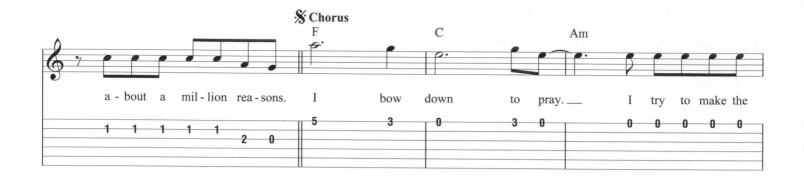

a - bout a mil - lion rea - sons. I bow down to pray. __ I try to make the

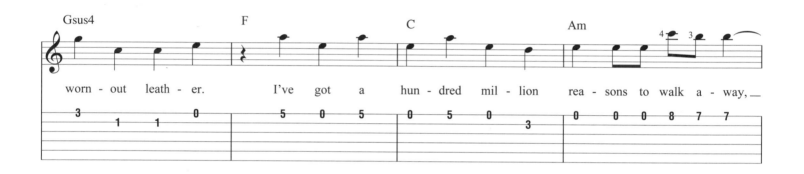

worst seem bet - ter. Lord, show me the way __ to cut through all this

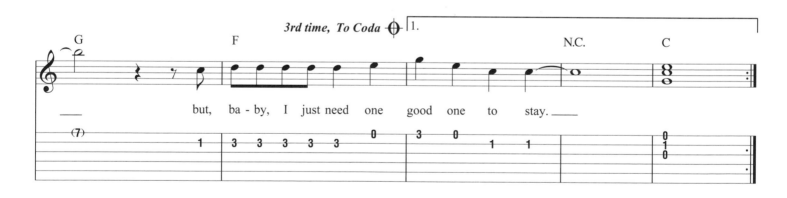

worn - out leath - er. I've got a hun - dred mil - lion rea - sons to walk a - way, __

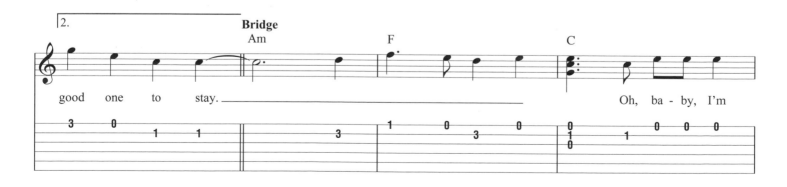

but, ba - by, I just need one good one to stay. __

good one to stay. ___ Oh, ba - by, I'm

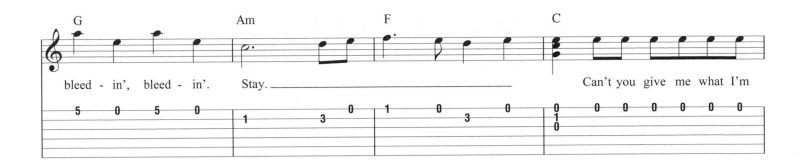

bleed - in', bleed - in'. Stay._____ Can't you give me what I'm

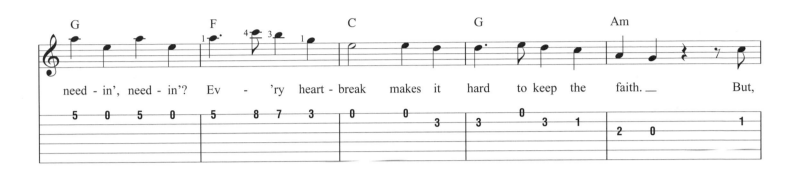

need - in', need - in'? Ev - 'ry heart - break makes it hard to keep the faith. __ But,

D.S. al Coda

ba - by, I just need one good one, good one, good one, good one, good one, good one. When

Coda

good one, good one. Tell me that you'll be the good one, good one.

Ba - by, I just need one good one to stay._____

29

Say You Won't Let Go

Words and Music by Steven Solomon, James Arthur and Neil Ormandy

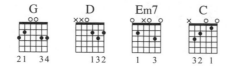

*Capo: III

Strum Pattern: 1
Pick Pattern: 5

Intro
Moderately

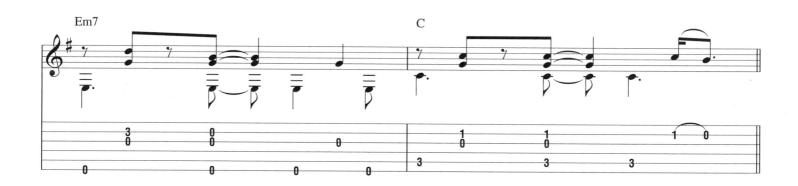

*Optional: To match recording, place capo at 3rd fret.

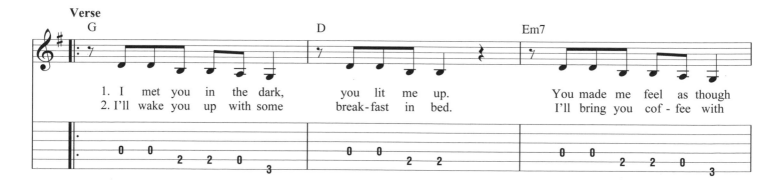

Verse

1. I met you in the dark, you lit me up. You made me feel as though
2. I'll wake you up with some break-fast in bed. I'll bring you cof-fee with

I was e - nough. _
a kiss on your head. _
We danced the night a - way,
I'll take the kids to school,
we drank too much,
wave them good - bye,

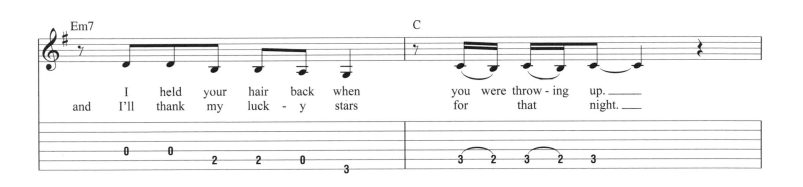

and
I held your hair back when
I'll thank my luck - y stars
you were throw - ing up. _
for that night. _

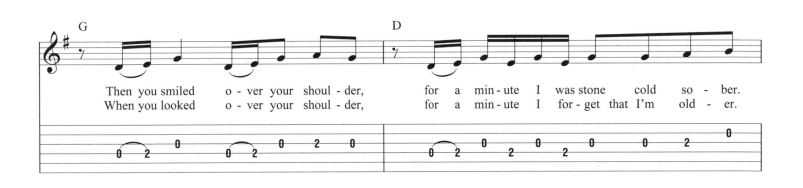

Then you smiled o - ver your shoul - der,
When you looked o - ver your shoul - der,
for a min - ute I was stone cold so - ber.
for a min - ute I for - get that I'm old - er.

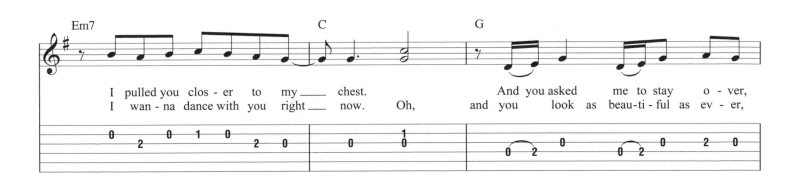

I pulled you clos - er to my _ chest.
I wan - na dance with you right _ now. Oh,
And you asked me to stay o - ver,
and you look as beau - ti - ful as ev - er,

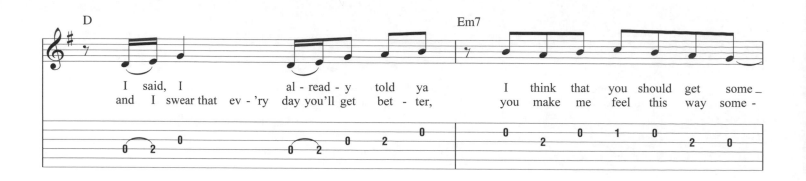

I said, I al - read - y told ya
and I swear that ev - 'ry day you'll get bet - ter,

I think that you should get some
you make me feel this way some -

Pre-Chorus

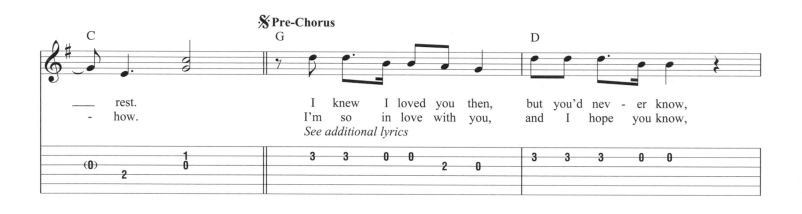

____ rest.
- how.

I knew I loved you then, but you'd nev - er know,
I'm so in love with you, and I hope you know,

See additional lyrics

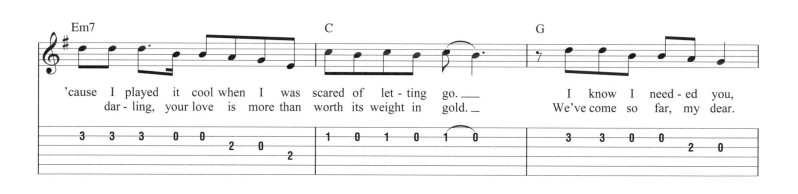

'cause I played it cool when I was scared of let - ting go. ___
dar - ling, your love is more than worth its weight in gold. __

I know I need - ed you,
We've come so far, my dear.

but I nev - er showed.
Look how we've grown.

But I wan - na stay with you un - til we're grey and old. __ }
And I wan - na stay with you un - til we're grey and old. __ }

Just

*Let chords ring, next 4 meas.

Additional Lyrics

Pre-Chorus: I'm gonna love you 'til my lungs give out,
I promise 'til death we part like in our vows.
So I wrote this song for you; how everybody knows
That it's just you and me until we're grey and old.

Send My Love (To Your New Lover)

Words and Music by Adele Adkins, Max Martin and Shellback

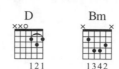

Strum Pattern: 1
Pick Pattern: 1

Intro
Moderately slow

*Chord symbols reflect implied harmony.

Verse

1. This was all you,___ none of it me.
2. I was too strong,_ you were trem-bling,

You put your hands on,___ on my bod-y and told___ me,
you could-n't han-dle ___ the hot heat ris-ing,

mm,___ you told me you were read-y for the big one,___ for the big jump,
mm,___ ba-by, I'm still ris-ing. I was run-ning,___ you were walk-ing,

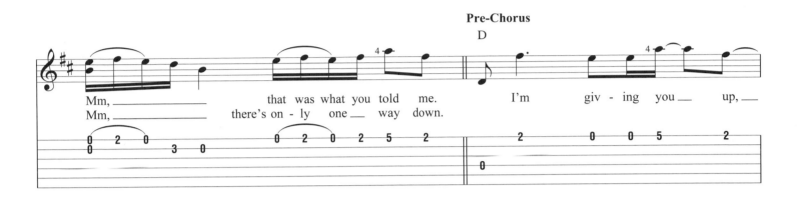

Pre-Chorus

Chorus

*Sung one octave higher.   **lover

Send my love to your new lo - ov - er, treat her bet - ter. We've

3rd time, To Coda ⊕

got - ta let go of all of our ghosts. We both know we ain't kids no more.___

1.

P.M.

2.

___ If you're read - y,___ if you're read - y, if you're read - y,___ I'm read - y.

If you're read - y,___ if you're read - y, we both know we ain't kids no more.___

Starboy

Words and Music by Abel Tesfaye, Guy-Manuel de Homem-Christo,
Thomas Bangalter, Henry Walter, Martin McKinney and Jason Quenneville

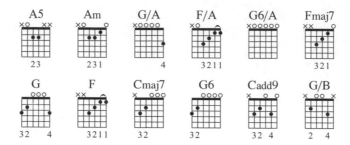

Strum Pattern: 1
Pick Pattern: 5

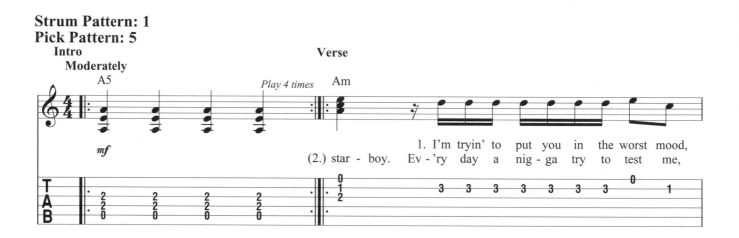

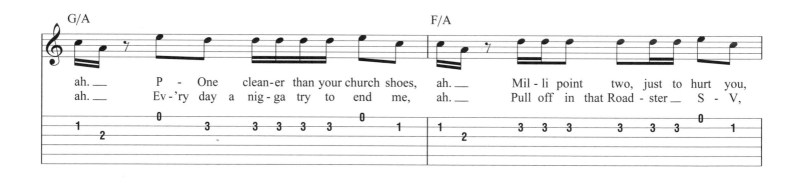

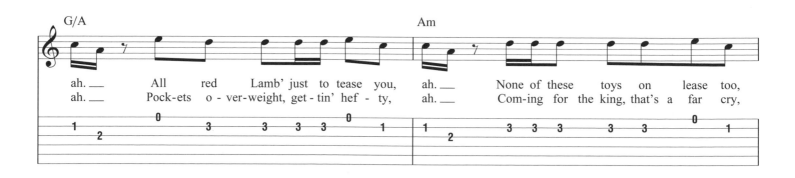

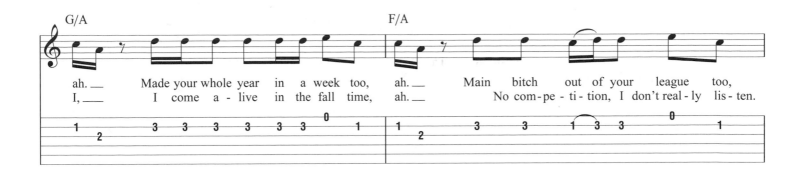

ah. ___ Made your whole year in a week too, ah. ___ Main bitch out of your league too,
I, ___ I come a-live in the fall time, ah. ___ No com-pe-ti-tion, I don't real-ly lis-ten.

Pre-Chorus

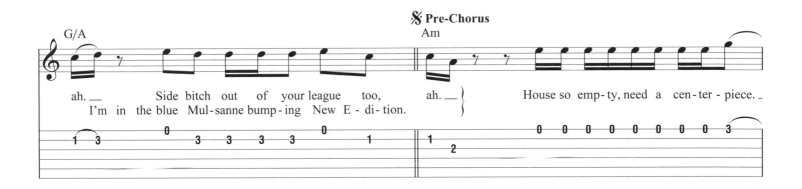

ah. ___ Side bitch out of your league too, ah. ___ House so emp-ty, need a cen-ter-piece. ___
I'm in the blue Mul-sanne bump-ing New E-di-tion.

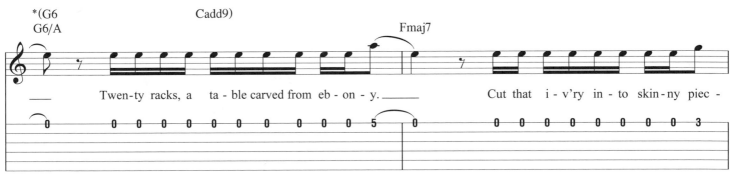

___ Twen-ty racks, a ta-ble carved from eb-on-y. _____ Cut that i-v'ry in-to skin-ny piec-

*3rd time, play chords in parens.

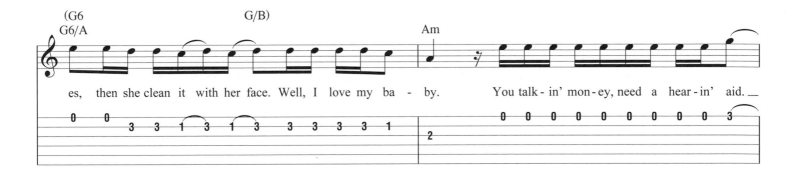

es, then she clean it with her face. Well, I love my ba-by. You talk-in' mon-ey, need a hear-in' aid. ___

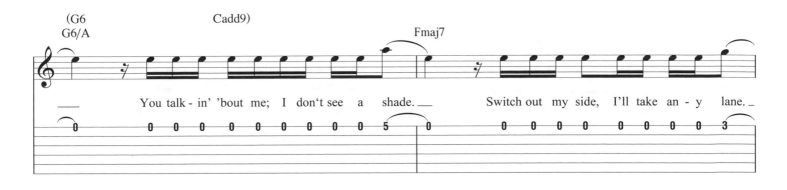

___ You talk-in' 'bout me; I don't see a shade. ___ Switch out my side, I'll take an-y lane. ___

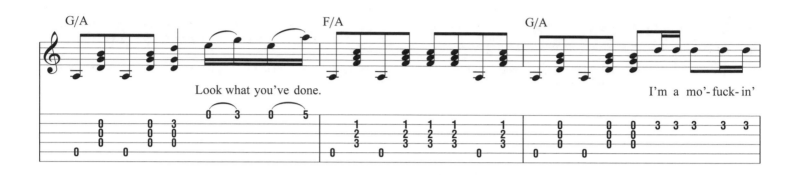

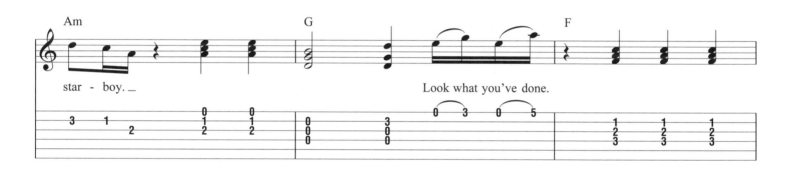

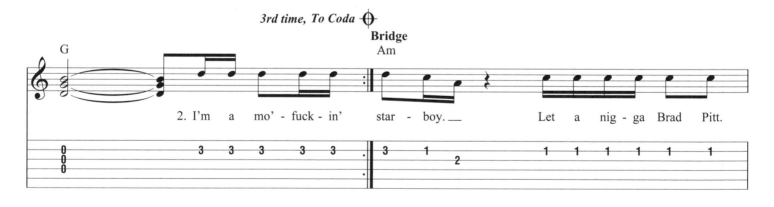

now she hit the gro-c'ry shop look-in' lav-ish. Star Trek groove in the Wrath of Khan. __

Girls get loose when they hear this song. ___ A hun-dred on the dash get me close to God. _ We don't

D.S. al Coda

pray for love; _ we just pray for cars. _____

Coda

Outro-Chorus

star - boy. __

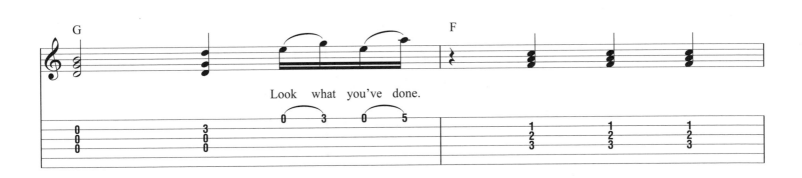

Look what you've done.

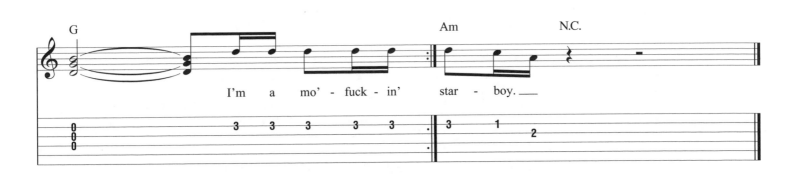

I'm a mo'-fuck-in' star - boy. __

This Town

Words and Music by Niall Horan, Michael Needle, Daniel Bryer and Jamie Scott

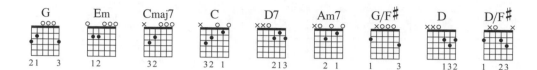

*Capo II

Strum Pattern: 1
Pick Pattern: 3

*Optional: To match recording, place capo at 2nd fret.

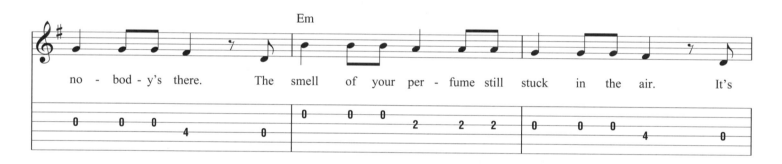

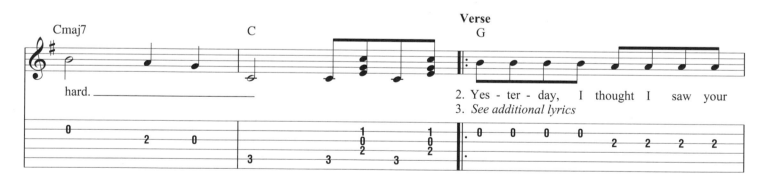

*Use Pattern 10   **Use Pattern 9

Additional Lyrics

3. I saw that you moved on with someone new.
   In the pub that we met, he's got his arms around you.
   It's so hard, so hard.

Treat You Better

Words and Music by Shawn Mendes, Scott Harris and Teddy Geiger

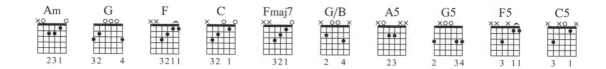

*Capo I

Strum Pattern: 6
Pick Pattern: 6

Intro
Moderately fast

*Optional: To match recording, place capo at 1st fret,

Verse

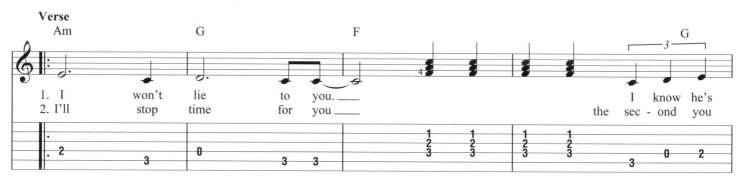

1. I won't lie to you. ___ I know he's
2. I'll stop time for you ___ the sec-ond you

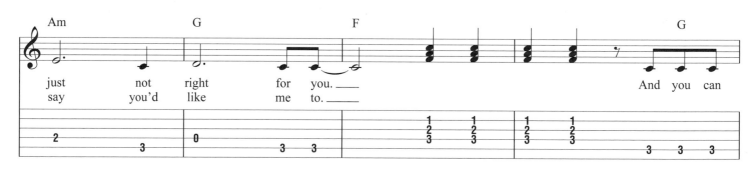

just not right for you. ___ And you can
say you'd like me to. ___

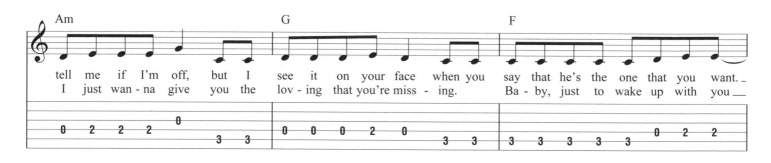

tell me if I'm off, but I see it on your face when you say that he's the one that you want. ___
I just wan-na give you the lov-ing that you're miss-ing. Ba-by, just to wake up with you ___

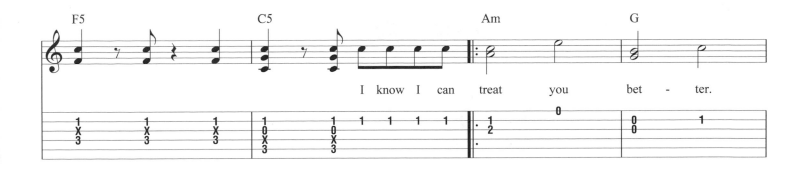

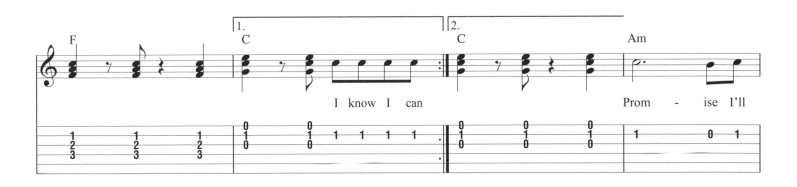

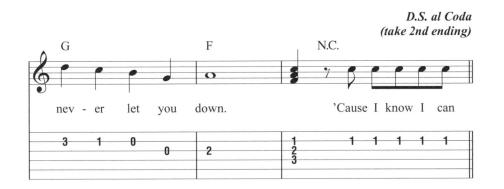

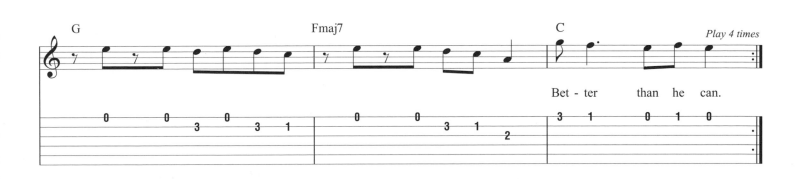

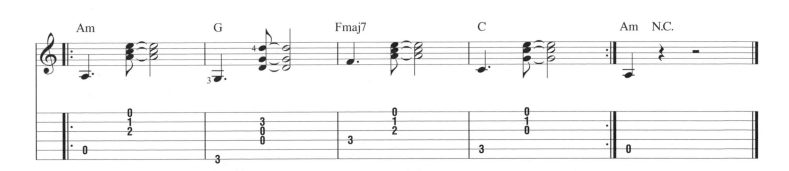

24K Magic

Words and Music by Bruno Mars, Philip Lawrence and Chris Brown

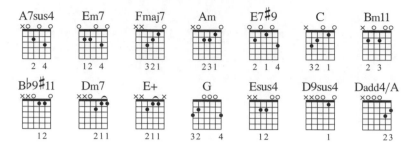

*Capo VIII

Strum Pattern: 1
Pick Pattern: 5

Intro
Freely

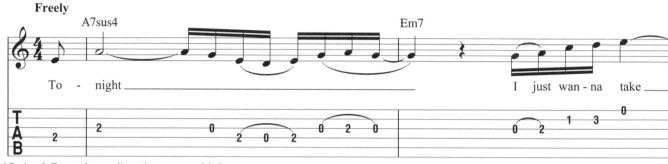

To - night _____ I just wan - na take _____

*Optional: To match recording, place capo on 8th fret.

_____ you high _____ er. Throw your _____ hands up in the sky. _____

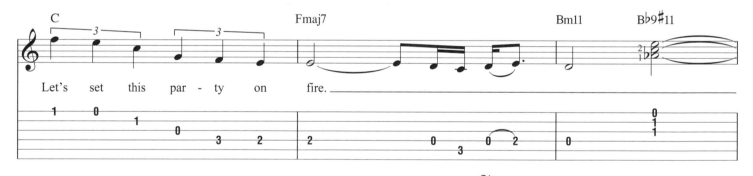

Let's set this par - ty on fire. _____

Moderately

%Chorus

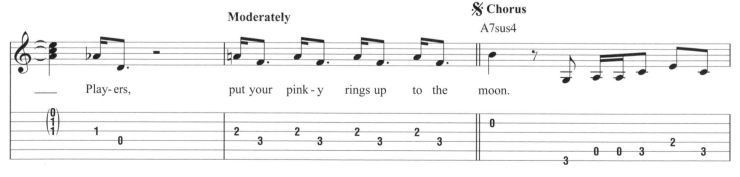

_____ Play- ers, put your pink - y rings up to the moon.

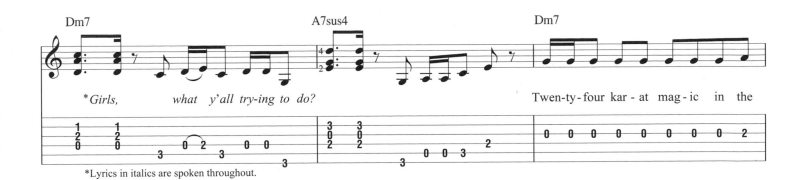

*Girls, what y'all try-ing to do? Twen-ty-four kar-at mag-ic in the

*Lyrics in italics are spoken throughout.

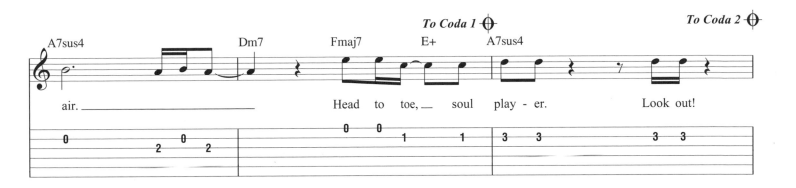

To Coda 1 ⊕   *To Coda 2* ⊕

air. _____ Head to toe, __ soul play-er. Look out!

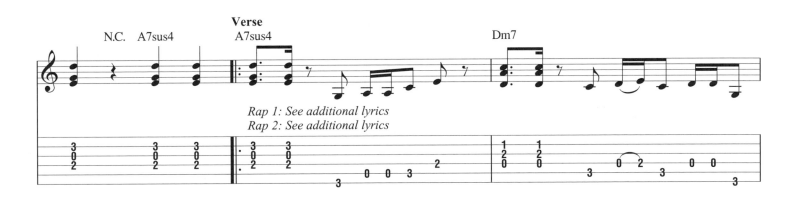

Verse

Rap 1: See additional lyrics
Rap 2: See additional lyrics

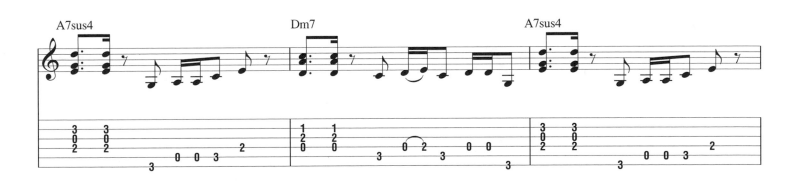

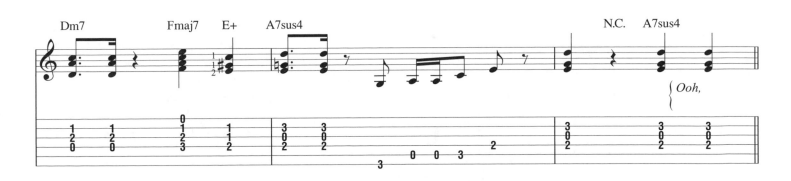

Ooh,

Pre-Chorus

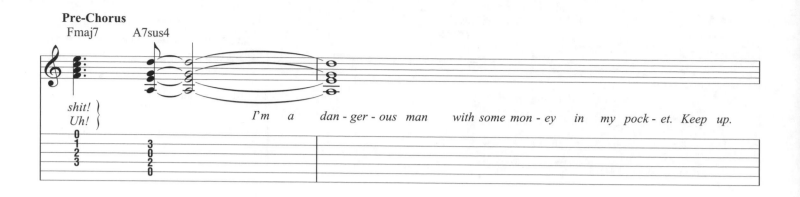

Fmaj7   A7sus4

shit! }
Uh! }   I'm a dan-ger-ous man with some mon-ey in my pock-et. Keep up.

Fmaj7   A7sus4

So man-y pret-ty girls a-round me and they're wak-ing up the rock-et. Keep up.

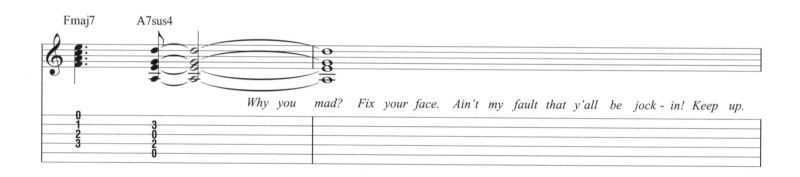

Fmaj7   A7sus4

Why you mad? Fix your face. Ain't my fault that y'all be jock-in! Keep up.

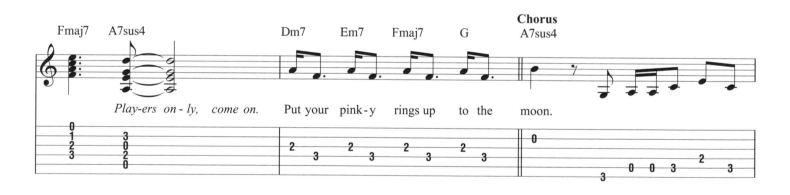

Fmaj7   A7sus4   Dm7   Em7   Fmaj7   G   **Chorus** A7sus4

Play-ers on-ly, come on. Put your pink-y rings up to the moon.

Dm7   A7sus4   Dm7

Girls, what y'all try-ing to do?   Twen-ty-four kar-at mag-ic in the

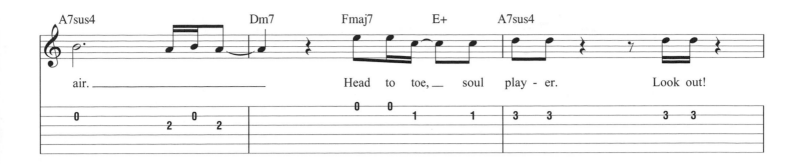

air. _____ Head to toe,__ soul play-er. Look out!

Bridge

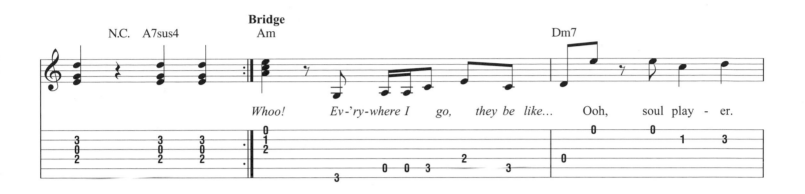

Whoo! Ev-'ry-where I go, they be like... Ooh, soul play-er.

Whoo! Ev-'ry-where I go, they be like... Ooh, soul play-er. *Whoo!* Ev-'ry-where I go, they be like...

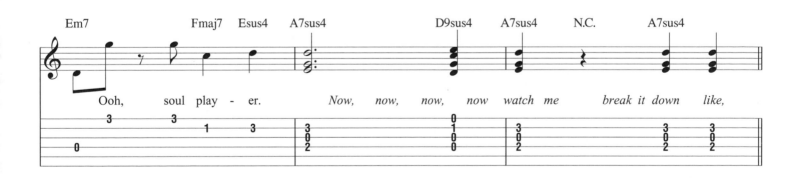

Ooh, soul play-er. *Now, now, now, now watch me break it down like,*

Interlude

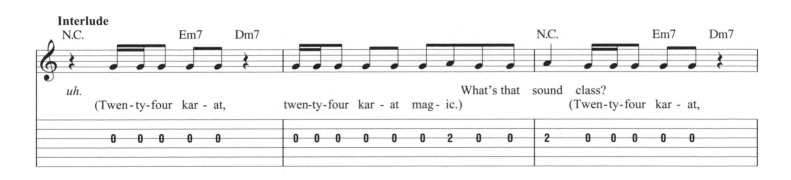

uh. (Twen-ty-four kar-at, twen-ty-four kar-at mag-ic.) What's that sound class? (Twen-ty-four kar-at,

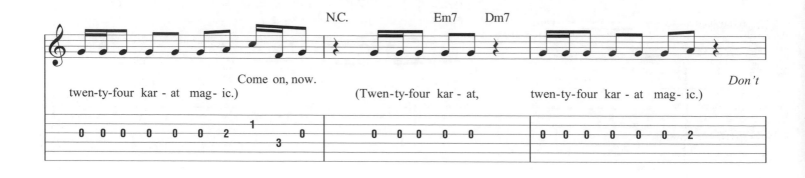

Come on, now.

twen-ty-four kar - at mag- ic.)   (Twen-ty-four kar - at,   twen-ty-four kar - at mag- ic.)

Don't

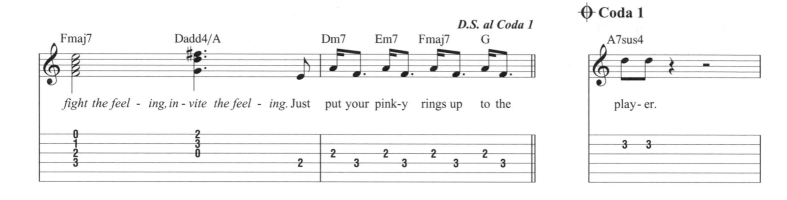

D.S. al Coda 1   🜋 **Coda 1**

fight the feel - ing, in - vite the feel - ing. Just   put your pink-y   rings up   to the   play- er.

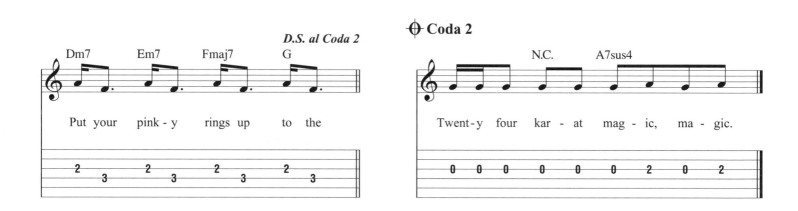

D.S. al Coda 2   🜋 **Coda 2**

Put your   pink - y   rings up   to the   Twent-y four kar - at mag - ic, ma - gic.

Additional Lyrics

Rap 1:   Pop, pop, it's show time (show time), show time (show time).
Guess who's back again.
Oh, they don't know? (Go on, tell 'em.)
They don't know? (Go on, tell 'em.)
I bet they know as soon as we walk in.
(Showin' up) wearin' Cuban links (yeah), designer minks (yeah),
Inglewood's finest shoes (whoop, whoop).
Don't look too hard; might hurt yourself.
Known to give the color red the blues.

Rap 2:   Second verse for the hustlers (hustlers), gangsters (gangsters),
Bad bitches and your ugly-ass friends.
Can I preach? (Uh-oh.) Can I preach? (Uh-oh.)
I gotta show 'em how a pimp get in.
First, take your sip (sip), do your dip (dip).
Spend your money like money ain't shit.
(Ooh, oh, we too fresh).
Got to blame it on Jesus (hash tag blessed).
They ain't ready for me.

EASY GUITAR WITH NOTES & TAB

This series features simplified arrangements with notes, tab, chord charts, and strum and pick patterns.

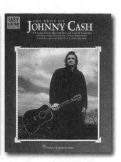

MIXED FOLIOS

00702287	Acoustic	$14.99
00702002	Acoustic Rock Hits for Easy Guitar	$12.95
00702166	All-Time Best Guitar Collection	$19.99
00699665	Beatles Best	$14.99
00702232	Best Acoustic Songs for Easy Guitar	$12.99
00119835	Best Children's Songs	$16.99
00702233	Best Hard Rock Songs	$14.99
00703055	The Big Book of Nursery Rhymes & Children's Songs	$14.99
00322179	The Big Easy Book of Classic Rock Guitar	$24.95
00698978	Big Christmas Collection	$16.95
00702394	Bluegrass Songs for Easy Guitar	$12.99
00703387	Celtic Classics	$14.99
00156245	Chart Hits of 2015-2016	$14.99
00702149	Children's Christian Songbook	$9.99
00702237	Christian Acoustic Favorites	$12.95
00702028	Christmas Classics	$7.95
00101779	Christmas Guitar	$14.99
00702185	Christmas Hits	$9.95
00702141	Classic Rock	$8.95
00702203	CMT's 100 Greatest Country Songs	$27.95
00702283	The Contemporary Christian Collection	$16.99
00702239	Country Classics for Easy Guitar	$19.99
00702282	Country Hits of 2009–2010	$14.99

00702257	Easy Acoustic Guitar Songs	$14.99
00702280	Easy Guitar Tab White Pages	$29.99
00702212	Essential Christmas	$9.95
00702041	Favorite Hymns for Easy Guitar	$9.95
00140841	4-Chord Hymns for Guitar	$7.99
00702281	4 Chord Rock	$10.99
00126894	Frozen	$14.99
00702286	Glee	$16.99
00699374	Gospel Favorites	$14.95
00122138	The Grammy Awards® Record of the Year 1958-2011	$19.99
00702160	The Great American Country Songbook	$16.99
00702050	Great Classical Themes for Easy Guitar	$8.99
00702116	Greatest Hymns for Guitar	$10.99
00702130	The Groovy Years	$9.95
00702184	Guitar Instrumentals	$9.95
00148030	Halloween Guitar Songs	$14.99
00702273	Irish Songs	$12.99
00702275	Jazz Favorites for Easy Guitar	$15.99
00702274	Jazz Standards for Easy Guitar	$15.99
00702162	Jumbo Easy Guitar Songbook	$19.99
00702258	Legends of Rock	$14.99
00702261	Modern Worship Hits	$14.99
00702189	MTV's 100 Greatest Pop Songs	$24.95
00702272	1950s Rock	$15.99
00702271	1960s Rock	$15.99

00702270	1970s Rock	$15.99
00702269	1980s Rock	$14.99
00702268	1990s Rock	$14.99
00109725	Once	$14.99
00702187	Selections from O Brother Where Art Thou?	$14.99
00702178	100 Songs for Kids	$14.99
00702515	Pirates of the Caribbean	$12.99
00702125	Praise and Worship for Guitar	$10.99
00702155	Rock Hits for Guitar	$9.95
00702285	Southern Rock Hits	$12.99
00702866	Theme Music	$12.99
00121535	30 Easy Celtic Guitar Solos	$14.99
00702220	Today's Country Hits	$9.95
00702198	Today's Hits for Guitar	$9.95
00121900	Today's Women of Pop & Rock	$14.99
00103626	Top Hits of 2012	$14.99
00702294	Top Worship Hits	$14.99
00702255	VH1's 100 Greatest Hard Rock Songs	$27.99
00702175	VH1's 100 Greatest Songs of Rock and Roll	$24.95
00702253	Wicked	$12.99

ARTIST COLLECTIONS

00702267	AC/DC for Easy Guitar	$15.99
00702598	Adele for Easy Guitar	$15.99
00702040	Best of the Allman Brothers	$14.99
00702865	J.S. Bach for Easy Guitar	$14.99
00702169	Best of The Beach Boys	$12.99
00702292	The Beatles — 1	$19.99
00125796	Best of Chuck Berry	$14.99
00702201	The Essential Black Sabbath	$12.95
02501615	Zac Brown Band — The Foundation	$16.99
02501621	Zac Brown Band — You Get What You Give	$16.99
00702043	Best of Johnny Cash	$16.99
00702263	Best of Casting Crowns	$12.99
00702090	Eric Clapton's Best	$10.95
00702086	Eric Clapton — from the Album Unplugged	$10.95
00702202	The Essential Eric Clapton	$14.99
00702250	blink-182 — Greatest Hits	$14.99
00702053	Best of Patsy Cline	$12.99
00702229	The Very Best of Creedence Clearwater Revival	$15.99
00702145	Best of Jim Croce	$15.99
00702278	Crosby, Stills & Nash	$12.99
00702219	David Crowder*Band Collection	$12.95
14042809	Bob Dylan	$14.99
00702276	Fleetwood Mac — Easy Guitar Collection	$14.99
00130952	Foo Fighters	$14.99
00139462	The Very Best of Grateful Dead	$14.99
00702136	Best of Merle Haggard	$12.99
00702227	Jimi Hendrix — Smash Hits	$14.99
00702288	Best of Hillsong United	$12.99
00702236	Best of Antonio Carlos Jobim	$12.95

00702245	Elton John — Greatest Hits 1970–2002	$14.99
00129855	Jack Johnson	$14.99
00702204	Robert Johnson	$10.99
00702234	Selections from Toby Keith — 35 Biggest Hits	$12.95
00702003	Kiss	$9.95
00110578	Best of Kutless	$12.99
00702216	Lynyrd Skynyrd	$15.99
00702182	The Essential Bob Marley	$12.95
00146081	Maroon 5	$14.99
00121925	Bruno Mars – Unorthodox Jukebox	$12.99
00702248	Paul McCartney — All the Best	$14.99
00702129	Songs of Sarah McLachlan	$12.95
00125484	The Best of MercyMe	$12.99
02501316	Metallica — Death Magnetic	$17.99
00702209	Steve Miller Band — Young Hearts (Greatest Hits)	$12.95
00124167	Jason Mraz	$14.99
00702096	Best of Nirvana	$14.99
00702211	The Offspring — Greatest Hits	$12.95
00138026	One Direction	$14.99
00702030	Best of Roy Orbison	$12.95
00702144	Best of Ozzy Osbourne	$14.99
00702279	Tom Petty	$12.99
00102911	Pink Floyd	$16.99
00702139	Elvis Country Favorites	$12.99
00702293	The Very Best of Prince	$12.99
00699415	Best of Queen for Guitar	$14.99
00109279	Best of R.E.M.	$14.99
00702208	Red Hot Chili Peppers — Greatest Hits	$12.95

00174793	The Very Best of Santana	$14.99
00702196	Best of Bob Seger	$12.95
00146046	Ed Sheeran	$14.99
00702252	Frank Sinatra — Nothing But the Best	$12.99
00702010	Best of Rod Stewart	$14.99
00702049	Best of George Strait	$14.99
00702259	Taylor Swift for Easy Guitar	$15.99
00702260	Taylor Swift — Fearless	$12.99
00139727	Taylor Swift — 1989	$17.99
00115960	Taylor Swift — Red	$16.99
00702290	Taylor Swift — Speak Now	$15.99
00702262	Chris Tomlin Collection	$14.99
00702226	Chris Tomlin — See the Morning	$12.95
00148643	Train	$14.99
00702427	U2 — 18 Singles	$14.99
00102711	Van Halen	$16.99
00702108	Best of Stevie Ray Vaughan	$14.99
00702123	Best of Hank Williams	$12.99
00702111	Stevie Wonder — Guitar Collection	$9.95
00702228	Neil Young — Greatest Hits	$15.99
00119133	Neil Young — Harvest	$14.99
00702188	Essential ZZ Top	$10.95

Prices, contents and availability subject to change without notice.

HAL•LEONARD®

Visit Hal Leonard online at
www.halleonard.com

0217

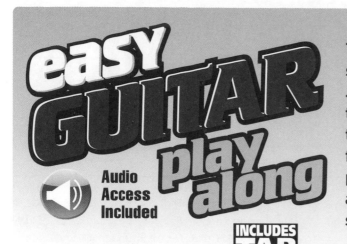

easy GUITAR play along

Audio Access Included

INCLUDES TAB

The **Easy Guitar Play Along**® series features streamlined transcriptions of your favorite songs. Just follow the tab, listen to the audio to hear how the guitar should sound, and then play along using the backing tracks. Playback tools are provided for slowing down the tempo without changing pitch and looping challenging parts. The melody and lyrics are included in the book so that you can sing or simply follow along.

1. ROCK CLASSICS

Jailbreak • Living After Midnight • Mississippi Queen • Rocks Off • Runnin' Down a Dream • Smoke on the Water • Strutter • Up Around the Bend.

00702560 Book/CD Pack....... $14.99

2. ACOUSTIC TOP HITS

About a Girl • I'm Yours • The Lazy Song • The Scientist • 21 Guns • Upside Down • What I Got • Wonderwall.

00702569 Book/CD Pack....... $14.99

3. ROCK HITS

All the Small Things • Best of You • Brain Stew (The Godzilla Remix) • Californication • Island in the Sun • Plush • Smells Like Teen Spirit • Use Somebody.

00702570 Book/CD Pack....... $14.99

4. ROCK 'N' ROLL

Blue Suede Shoes • I Get Around • I'm a Believer • Jailhouse Rock • Oh, Pretty Woman • Peggy Sue • Runaway • Wake Up Little Susie.

00702572 Book/CD Pack....... $14.99

6. CHRISTMAS SONGS

Have Yourself a Merry Little Christmas • A Holly Jolly Christmas • The Little Drummer Boy • Run Rudolph Run • Santa Claus Is Comin' to Town • Silver and Gold • Sleigh Ride • Winter Wonderland.

00101879 Book/CD Pack......... $14.99

7. BLUES SONGS FOR BEGINNERS

Come On (Part 1) • Double Trouble • Gangster of Love • I'm Ready • Let Me Love You Baby • Mary Had a Little Lamb • San-Ho-Zay • T-Bone Shuffle.

00103235 Book/CD Pack........ $14.99

8. ACOUSTIC SONGS FOR BEGINNERS

Barely Breathing • Drive • Everlong • Good Riddance (Time of Your Life) • Hallelujah • Hey There Delilah • Lake of Fire • Photograph.

00103240 Book/CD Pack $14.99

9. ROCK SONGS FOR BEGINNERS

Are You Gonna Be My Girl • Buddy Holly • Everybody Hurts • In Bloom • Otherside • The Rock Show • Santa Monica • When I Come Around.

00103255 Book/CD Pack.....$14.99

10. GREEN DAY

Basket Case • Boulevard of Broken Dreams • Good Riddance (Time of Your Life) • Holiday • Longview • 21 Guns • Wake Me up When September Ends • When I Come Around.

00122322 Book/CD Pack $14.99

11. NIRVANA

All Apologies • Come As You Are • Heart Shaped Box • Lake of Fire • Lithium • The Man Who Sold the World • Rape Me • Smells Like Teen Spirit.

00122325 Book/ Online Audio $14.99

12. TAYLOR SWIFT

Fifteen • Love Story • Mean • Picture to Burn • Red • We Are Never Ever Getting Back Together • White Horse • You Belong with Me.

00122326 Book/CD Pack $16.99

13. AC/DC

Back in Black • Dirty Deeds Done Dirt Cheap • For Those About to Rock (We Salute You) • Hells Bells • Highway to Hell • Rock and Roll Ain't Noise Pollution • T.N.T. • You Shook Me All Night Long.

14042895 Book/ Online Audio........$16.99

14. JIMI HENDRIX – SMASH HITS

All Along the Watchtower • Can You See Me • Crosstown Traffic • Fire • Foxey Lady • Hey Joe • Manic Depression • Purple Haze • Red House • Remember • Stone Free • The Wind Cries Mary.

00130591 Book/ Online Audio........$24.99

HAL•LEONARD®
www.halleonard.com

Prices, contents, and availability subject to change without notice.